Let's Write!

A No-Nonsense Manual

by Melanie Stiles

Christian Life Coach

Blue Jean Coach Publishing
Houston, Texas

Blue Jean Coach Publishing
109 N. Post Oak Lane, Ste. 525
Houston, Texas 77024
USA

Access other books by Melanie
or contact her at:
Melanie@MelanieStiles.com
www.MelanieStiles.com

ISBN: 978-1493570300

Contents

"And God *is* able to make all grace abound toward you, that you, always having all sufficiency in all *things*, may have an abundance for every good work." 2 Corinthians 9:8 (NKJV)

Introduction

As a frequent speaker at writers' conferences, I am asked one particular question at every event. *Melanie, exactly how do I get this writing/publishing thing started?* I have never been able to give an adequate answer in the limited amount time I am allowed to spend with individuals inside these venues. Typically, I resort to offering my email address with a promise to reply to inquiries. Unfortunately, I think all parties walk away feeling less than satiated.

After I return home, I often mull over how a minute conversation can accomplish what is essentially impossible. One thing I have continually resolved is this: **IT IS A QUESTION THAT DESERVES A COMPREHENSIVE ANSWER.**

The writing/publishing world can mirror that of the Internal Revenue Service requirements for filing an income tax return. Both scenarios seem to contain hidden rules and regulations. There are popular fallacies floating around in each, lending confusion to what we already presumed could be ascertained as fact. These factors can often cause an unprepared beginner (and truthfully, at times, even those of us who are a bit more advanced) to throw up our hands in despair and question whether or not we should even attempt to write for publication.

Experience has caused me to believe the tool that would be most beneficial to the beginning writer is a primer, much like the small volumes we read when we attended kindergarten. Do you remember those simple, yet easy to understand, stories that possibly opened your world to the eventual dream of wanting to create your own manuscripts? Perhaps it was a different experience that ignited the fire within the writing portion of your soul. Either way, this primer – this small introductory book about entering what I consider to be a magnificent world – strives to give you the very basic, bare-bones components you will need to accomplish your goals.

I've been writing my story since the first time I dabbled in poetry as an anxiety-ridden teenager. I learned to relish the act of presenting my woes, and gradually all other aspects of life, in written form. I didn't dream of publishing my work until a much later date. When I matured enough to realize God was in the gift giving business and I had received the heart of a scribe, I walked into the maze in which we all stand – the labyrinth of writing to completion with the intent to inherit a byline. I learned by God's grace and through kind and wonderful people He led into my midst, folks who persistently instructed and interacted with me along the way.

My process began in the '80s. The industry has exploded in a myriad of ways since the days of the typewriter. In spite of the changes, I have written and published hundreds of projects. It might also be relevant for you to know I still practice what is written within these pages regularly. Years of navigation have brought me to the solemn understanding God's gifts are meant to be passed along to others, and to do otherwise would be a waste of both His efforts and my own life. I believe all writers have a purpose within His Kingdom.

Over time, my craft and marketing skills have drastically improved. Even so, I expect to be able to repeat this same statement a few years from now. And then again, a few years after that. As we grow and change, so do our words.

It is my hope and sincere prayer that I can be one of many divine connections He has for you. There is no question as to whether or not I will cover everything you may want to know. Omniscience belongs only to One. I will, however, make this offer. The copyright page of this book details my contact information. Ask away! I will do my best to help you along your journey.

Blessings and keep writing,

Melanie Stiles

1

No-Nonsense Principle One:
Take a Good Look at YOU

"Happy is the man that findeth wisdom,
and the man that getteth understanding.
Proverbs 3:13 (KJV)

This is apt to be the only principle you'll seriously entertain the notion of skipping, as its relevance isn't immediately clear when it comes to exploring your success. You might be tempted to think, *"Why bother? I already know who I am, don't I?"* Please don't listen! It is Principle One for the most important of reasons.

Vision and reality often have two entirely different definitions. It is absolutely necessary to bring BOTH into clear focus to achieve success. Vision might be thought of as the place you intend to go, while reality is the place in which you now stand. You can see the evident separation between the two in unbidden exclamations such as, "I'm writing the next bestseller right now! Would you like me to speak to your group?" This is a visioneering-type statement that takes no account of the reality component called credibility. Is it true that some first time novelists are touched by the favor of God? Of course! Interestingly enough, I've never heard or read about a pre-announcement by any of them. Even overnight sensation authors had to adhere to publishing industry guidelines. They also understand that credibility has to be earned first, mainly by completing and publishing a book. This is usually done prior to gaining audience before fellow writers.

The key component in the question, "How do I get started?"

is the word, "I." This first step on your writing journey is designed to help you **realistically** evaluate who you are as a writer today. Recognizing your own strengths, weaknesses, time constraints and unconscious habits are integral to the placement of relevant parameters, which can cause your project action plans to be greatly simplified. It's imperative to acknowledge you – the writer – so you can aptly determine your next direction development. Your work in this Principle is step one in bringing your reality into alignment with your vision.

Sacrifice whatever it takes to honestly answer the questions below. If you can finish the list to your satisfaction in a day, then move on to No-Nonsense Principle Two. If you've not addressed your own self-awareness in a while, don't beat yourself up for taking the time you need to think about the questions. If you aren't sure about your own behavior, ask a close friend. Your primary focus is NOT correct or incorrect answers. In fact, there are no wrong responses. There are only truthful ones. It will be helpful to record your thoughts inside a notebook or journal so you can refer back to them as you read further. You didn't get to write in your kindergarten books either, did you? Your answers will directly correspond to ensuing information in the rest of this manual. Let's get started.

Self-Exploration Questions
Please Complete All Questions at This Time

No-Nonsense Principle Two
Self-Exploration Questions

2-1. Are you able to capture snapshots of life in a few descriptive words?

2-2. Are you able to clearly see the connection between scripture and your own life experiences?

2-3. Do you have a lot to say or an intense passion around one topic in particular?

2-4. Do you currently write in short bursts or longer intense sessions?

No-Nonsense Principle Three
Self-Exploration Questions

3-1. Do you regularly set goals for yourself and follow through?

3-2. Do you take information from any source as gospel or are you inclined to dig a little deeper?

3-3. Do you gather the right tools for any job?

3-4. Would you rate your organizational skills as low, medium or high?

No-Nonsense Principle Four
Self-Exploration Questions

4-1. Do you consider yourself a social person or an introvert, preferring to avoid others?

4-2. Do you have an internal discernment about the needs of others, or do you expect people to state their requests?

4-3. Do you prefer one particular age range to others?

4-4. Are you more storyteller or problem solver?

No-Nonsense Principle Five
Self-Exploration Questions

5-1. Are you able to avoid distractions and travel from Point A to Point Z directly when planning and executing the actions necessary for the completion of a project?

5-2. Can you envision a step-by-step process?

5-3. Can you create appropriately sequenced to-do lists or do you take one step, then stop to figure out the next?

5-4. Do you naturally have the fortitude to stick with a project during duress, stress or distraction?

No-Nonsense Principle Six
Self-Exploration Questions

6-1. How much time do you spend in prayer about your projects?

6-2. Can you thrive in a team/group environment?

6-3. How do you respond to constructive criticism?

6-4. Are you able to communicate well with strangers about information that is important to you?

Congratulations! You're done! Take heart in this quote by John Eldredge (author, counselor and Christianity lecturer), "The fear of the Lord is the beginning of knowledge, but the end of knowledge is the courage to act."

2

No-Nonsense Principle Two:
There Are Many Ways to Tell Your Story

"You make known to me the path of life; you will fill me with
joy in your presence, with eternal pleasures at your right hand."
Psalm 16:11 (NIV)

Principle Two is about defining a few industry terms that
connect the length of a manuscript to its appropriate destination.
All publishers have specialized guidelines, but these generalities
will give you an overall view of size.

Book Lengths

Novels for the adult market are written in varying word
lengths and with specificity to the publishing house that
purchases them. However, on the chance you are considering a
self-publishing route, certain guidelines should still be in place
so that you demonstrate professionalism. It is important to
remember that word count relates to production costs on both
fronts.

Here are some overall word counts to consider:

Below 80K is generally considered too short (but could fall
into the Novella category).
80K-90K stands as the general guideline for a novel word
count.
Over 90K can be viewed as too long, except in particular

genres (see below).

Young Adult Fiction averages 55K-70K words.

Children's Fiction gets more complicated as the length of a manuscript essentially depends on the age range of your audience. The best way to determine how long your work should be is to spend a morning in your public library reading what you intend to write. You might also take note as to what publishing houses produced your favorites.

Memoirs follow the guidelines given above for novels.

Nonfiction Books are all over the map, given varying content. Gift books fall under this category, and design plays a huge factor within this genre. Singular topic nonfiction titles can commonly be found in the 50K word count range. Again, researching your own passion zone is recommended.

Sci-Fi/Fantasy tends to make exception to the novel rule above with average lengths extending to as much as 115K and beyond. Again, research, research, research!

Articles and Blogs

Articles come in all shapes and sizes. The distinction between online publishing and hard copy publishing needs to be understood when considering selling or even creating a branding blog base. Key words to remember for online are: short, tightly written, early hook. Feature articles are manuscripts meant to be centerpieces of a publication; however, the centerpiece of a website is quite different from the layout in a major magazine. If you want to write for a particular magazine or site, review their word count requirements and subject matter history prior to "pitching" your idea.

Devotionals are popular choices for new Christian writers. Please notice that each publication has its own preference in format, Bible translation and theme. Quite a few devotional publications require you to write samples and send them in for a possible assignment. It's important to note that breaking the rules will only get you tossed into the waste bin. Professional writers navigate the guidelines.

Blog Posts have better success if staged in the 250-300 word range. Keep in mind how long you look at a site or how many lines you read before you click out to something else. This makes your first three sentences prime real estate. They have to capture or "hook" your reader and inspire them to read further. Of course, there are some exceptions, such as technical sites that actually require longer pieces. Also, blogs provide an avenue for the creation of audio/visual appeal through picture, video posts and podcasts.

Poetry

Poetry is a snapshot. A moment in time, thought or deed. As such, there are plenty of markets that accept and pay for poetry. Another outlet to consider is contests, but a word of warning is necessary. Not all contests are legitimate and you should do your homework by checking out the sponsoring company. Sometimes simply Googling the contest and adding the word "scam" is enough. Another website that is helpful is www.winningwriters.com. Minimal entry fees are fine, but you should NEVER pay to include your poem in any book.

I feel obligated to use a cliché here, which is essentially a major writer no-no! Still, the truth is often wrapped inside those lovely overused phrases, so here goes. The rules and standards above will get you through, for the most part, but there will be times as you move through your writing career when "the rules are made to be broken." My advice to you is to travel well within previously established territory before you step out into "against the grain" decisions.

Attributes of a Professional Writer

It is amazing how professionalism can send your work up to the top of the slush pile. There are a number of items an editor has a right to expect when he picks up a manuscript, and we accentuate our own reputation when we deal with them from the onset.

Grammar/punctuation excellence is an absolute must. That may mean you will need to invest in a course or read a book to improve your skills. The term "writer" implies you already know how to place words in an appropriate order with the correct punctuation. There will always be nuances we will have to learn, but a document that is littered with errors says you didn't care enough about your own words to review them from a grammatical standpoint. You can play with your grammar at www.funenglishgames.com.

Guidelines are followed to the letter by a writer who is truly seeking publication. To do less is to tell the editor that you overrode the opinion of both his expertise and his publication.

Professionals let their work speak for itself because they already understand it is their own writing ability they are selling. Many new writers will try to pursue markets by writing query letters attempting to persuade an editor based on personal character cheerleading, instead of outlining the strengths of their piece. Listing credits and being positive are certainly necessary, but bribery is impossible.

Let's Review No-Nonsense Principle Two
Self-Explorations

2.1 If you are a writer who is able to capture snapshots of life, consider poetry. Not every writer can encapsulate tiny moments in micro fashion. You have a gift!

2.2 If you are a person who connects life application to scripture, consider writing devotionals or other spiritual help pieces. Even though you'll have to try out for most markets by submitting samples, your gift will make a way for you!

2.3 If you are a sole intention person, consider starting with smaller articles and blogs about your unique passion subject. After you have mastered those venues, the book in your heart will nearly write itself. If you have a freelancer's passion, everything has the potential to interest you. Always consider your long-term reputation before agreeing to write on any topic.

2.4 Writing in short bursts or longer intense sessions delineates what type of writing schedule you will want to pursue. Either way, it will, at some point, be necessary to write for the sake of writing rather than when the urge of inspiration hits you. Writers write. They write often. They write whether they feel like writing or not. It is what builds a career. It is often more advantageous for a new writer to start small on the way to the book. You can graduate from small to intermediate and long-term writing goals.

3

No-Nonsense Principle Three:
Bring Along Good Baggage

Let us examine our ways and test them,
and let us return to the Lord.
Lamentations 3:40 (NIV)

We all have a few things already packed away for the journey to publication. The question every beginning writer has to ask is essentially, *"Do I have the basic tools to write what I want to write?"* Many writers want to believe all they absolutely require is the story nestled within their own heads.

Think, instead, of your story as merely the tip of a writing iceberg. It takes some girth beneath any article, poem or book to make it worthwhile. Below is a short list of items a writer would do well to accumulate early. At first, the items may appear to be costly and will most certainly take some energy to collect. Keep in mind that resale book shops and Amazon used books are perfectly acceptable for garnering first-class materials at deep discounts.

After you've collected everything on the list, don't prematurely decide you're done. Expect to chase aspects of the craft for as long as you write. All the best writers do! In addition to the elementary reference library below, you'll need to make one more simple commitment: **READ ONE BOOK ON THE CRAFT OF WRITING EVERY THREE MONTHS.** If you can stick to this simple practice, your knowledge will continue to increase indefinitely.

A Writer's Reference Baggage

A nice, fat dictionary leads the pack when suggesting reference materials. Don't be tempted to depend on the online versions. They work well if you know the exact word you want to check, but online sites leave no room for leafing through in inquisitive exploration. All writers should have a curiosity about words in general. It's harder to appease the urge without seeing copious lists of words on the pages of an actual book.

A rhyming dictionary is a must for a poet intent on writing beyond free verse.

A crossword dictionary works as a synonym finder, as well as contributing to a lovely writer's pastime. It's easy to install additional enticing, valuable vocabulary into your word bank with a puzzle a day!

A synonym finder is an absolute necessity for every writer. I, of course, have a favorite, titled *The Synonym Finder*, by J.I. Rodale (see resource list). The back cover touts the book as "the last word in thesauruses." Or use www.thesaurus.com.

Writer's Market by *Writer's Digest* is a major staple needed to sell your work. These books are published annually, but the current year's edition is not absolutely necessary. There are changes that occur in the publishing field every year that don't make it into the existing issue. And yet we survive. A market guide will steer you into the particulars of where your work might fit, but you will still have to use website/guideline instructions to finish the job. That makes any writer's market only the beginning of a process. *Writer's Digest* publishes many "*Market*" formats for specific genres including songwriters, poets and children's markets.

For most magazine publications, it is also necessary to order back issues and study themes, topics covered, writing style, ads and presentation. The information on how to do so is included in each particular entry within the *Writer's Market* where applicable. Think of the book as a directory to let you know what is out there. Many writers are pleased to discover markets they wouldn't normally have had an awareness of otherwise. Two years in arrears is still an acceptable market guide to use (e.g., 2012 or 2013 at the time this guide was published). Anything older risks your spending time chasing markets that might not exist anymore. The industry is ever changing. The most important part of owning and using this book is to read carefully and recognize it as only a beginning source of researching any publication.

The *Christian Writer's Market Guide* is a specific guide for writers intent on publishing in the Christian arena. Writers interested in publishing prayers, devotionals and particular denomination manuscripts would benefit from this purchase. It is worth your time to read it through from cover to cover to acquaint yourself with all aspects of this segment of the writing industry.

The *Chicago Manual of Style* is the industry's grammar and punctuation standard for both fiction and nonfiction books (with the exception of scholarly publications). It certainly belongs on your bookshelf, but it can be a bit overwhelming at first.

Eats, Shoots & Leaves by **Lynne Truss,** might be a better and more humorous grammatical guide approach for those who are intimidated by *The Chicago Manual of Style* listed above.

I mentioned previously that many writers mistakenly believe the only tool required is the story in their head. Think, also, about a book bought, but pages never visited. Owning this beginning library is a waste of time unless your intentions are to access them at appropriate times during your writing career. Only you can make the decision to be diligent.

The Best Baggage Is Within

A writer's best baggage comes from within. This excellent luggage can't be purchased, but resides within the heart, spirit and mind. Writing is not a fairytale existence, as is nothing else on the planet. Your individual scribe-like journey is apt to resemble the rest of your life – full of good days and peppered with not-so-good ones. If you're like most writers, the temptations to give up, celebrate and stand fast will and can be wrapped up in small measures of time. In those less than stellar moments, you're going to have to reach down inside to find something to hold on to. It should help to review characteristics and behaviors that will ease the way.

Integrity should go without saying, but in the worst of times, any writer might be tempted to use the work of others to gain what they believe could be a step up. Of course, plagiarism is much more than a step back. It is blight, once danced with, one would find extremely difficult to overcome. Remember average apprenticeship is in the neighborhood of ten years before we begin to gain ground on a regular basis through our own audience and abilities. We have to realize God only gives shortcuts. He, alone, can move you forward faster with one touch of His favor. That is the only Source of increase beyond our own work we should seek. Proverbs 10:9 (NKJ) says, "He who walks with integrity walks securely, but he who perverts his ways will become known."

Credibility simply means you need to be able to stand as an expert behind your publications. Some fields will, by necessity, require more educational pedigree than others.

Picture this. You've decided the tree limb that slaps the roof of your house has to go today. The branch does not have a wide circumference, so a quick snip with your hand-held hedge trimmer ought to do the trick. You haul out the ladder and make the climb. Somehow, now that you're fifteen feet above ground, the job looks a little more difficult. You are no quitter and set about attacking the task with a vengeance. Deep in the throes of woody war, you fail to recognize the thrust you used has now exceeded the narrow limits of the step on the ladder. With a robust shout, down you go! Unfortunately, you are colliding, rather quickly, with the rocks you used to line the edge of your flowerbed. Even in the midst of the confusion, your ears pick up on the muffled snap that escapes from your left arm, just before you begin to assimilate an incredibly sharp pain.

Your neighbor has been watering his roses and not really minding his own business. Your sudden dethroning has not gone unseen. He drops the hose and crosses the street at sprinter speeds.

"Are you okay?" he asks with genuine concern.

Through eyesight now filled intermittently with blinking constellations, you manage to respond with fair assurance that you have broken a bone.

"Why, I just finished my first aid class for the Boy Scout troop," he says excitedly. "I can splint that thing in no time! We got this!"

Would you humor your neighbor, or unashamedly beg him to drive you to the nearest emergency clinic?

Credibility matters. It creates a reassurance for your reader that your words are trustworthy. Think through what forms of credibility are necessary for your writing area. If you don't have what you need, get it.

Organization is a behavior relating directly to professionalism. To consider writing as a career choice (even part-time) is to consider it a business. No editor expects to have to forgive a manuscript submitted outside guidelines, after deadline or with coffee stains on the corner of the cover letter. A departing manuscript must always be dressed in best form. In addition, it is not unusual for editors to ask for resource confirmation of particular information within a piece. Keeping your records in order will provide you with the ability to access everything you need quickly. A rapid, concise response could mean the difference between a sale and a rejection.

Accountability involves the ability to say what you mean and follow through accordingly. It is a character trait so directly linked to your growth, Jesus speaks to it in the parable of the talents. The accountability point lies in Matthew 25:23 (NKJ): "His lord said to him, 'Well done, good and faithful servant; you have been faithful over a few things, I will make you ruler over many things. Enter into the joy of your lord.'" One act of accountability leads to another, which will create a history of good writing habits. These habits will, in turn, foster the handling of multiple deadlines and writing projects.

Patience is the capacity to tolerate delay, trouble or suffering without getting angry, frustrated or upset. Additionally, patience seems to be misconstrued as something other than a quality or character trait intended to be developed. How many people have you heard to make the statement, "Oh, I just don't have patience," as if this is an unchanging fact in one's life. Truth can be brutal for some, and please take this sobering truth with genuine love coupled around it. You will need patience more than any other baggage listed thus far. It will be the thing you can lean on through ugly adverbs and raw rejections. I keep the apostle Paul's self-awareness advice close during challenging situations. Philippians 4:11-13 (NKJ) (repeated out loud): "Not that I speak in regard to need, for I have learned in whatever state I am, to be content: I know how to be abased, and I know how to abound. Everywhere and in all things I have learned both to be full and to be hungry, both to abound and to suffer need. I can do all things through Christ who strengthens me." Remember you're only living in one small part of your life each day. Only God sees where your next moment of celebration lies. It could be closer than you imagine!

Passion given by God is a wonderful gift, but the enemy knows his job. Beware of his tactics called self-doubt, questioning and low self-esteem meant to dampen, disparage and disrupt the message you were intended to give the world. If you are called to write, there is nothing more to entertain. There is only growth and work to be done. Your God-given passion is the inner strength that forever guides you from one level to the next in your calling.

Perseverance goes without saying in a writer's journey, but what does need to be mentioned is how it is accomplished only in a deep and abiding relationship with God. Galatians 6:9 (RSV) shows that He expects the processes in our writing world to contain challenges. The scripture forewarns us: "And let us not grow weary in well-doing, for in due season we shall reap, if we do not lose heart." Since your gift comes from Him, doesn't it make sense that only He can truly understand your struggles within it?

Prayer is the core of our good baggage. Prayer causes everything else listed here to take on life. I find it surprising that many new writers don't add daily confessions concerning their craft to prayer and meditation periods. Here is my personal favorite. I suggest you find your own. Of course, standing on more than one scripture is even more enriching.

Use 2 Corinthians 9:8 (NIV) as a personal daily confession... "And **God is able to bless MY WRITING EFFORTS abundantly**, so that in all things at all times, **HAVING ALL THAT I NEED**, I will abound in every good work."

Writer, Phyllis A. Whitney, says, "You must want to enough. Enough to take all the rejections, enough to pay the price of disappointment and discouragement while you are learning. Like any other artist you must learn your craft – then you can add all the genius you like."

Let's Review No-Nonsense Principle Three
Self- Explorations

3.1 Setting goals in the form of writing deadlines can make or break a potential writing career. Unless you've signed a contract, you will have to function in the discipline of self-demand. Deadlines give your project validity. Validity creates momentum. Momentum will get your manuscript completed and to a market.

3.2 Never accept information without first considering its source. Perspective directly connects a story to how much truth is contained therein. Think about the people in your life who overly exaggerate incidents vs. those who barely divulge more than a few insignificant details. Somewhere in the middle is usually where truth is nestled. It's up to you, the writer, to discover what matters.

3.3 Impatience breeds insufficient material, research and editing in a manuscript. There are many times, particularly for poets, when it can be required to check the definition of every single word in the body of a poem to ensure you have said precisely what you intended to say. To assume you are better than the craft process is to assume your ego has overridden your wisdom. Tell yourself frequently that you operate in God's timing and not your own. In the simplest of terms – it takes as long as it takes. Isn't your goal excellence?

3.4 We talked about organization above, but here are some specific guidelines that might help. Don't over clutter your workspace with nonessential items. Many writers have a secret wish to own a Staples store. Resist the urge and keep it simple. File storage is a must. If you are a paperless person, be sure to back up on flash drives or clouds. Keep your files inclusive with final submission, published copy and payment records. Create a tax record filing system and update monthly, recording and stowing away expense and income receipts. If you rated yourself as low in this skillset, enlist someone who is highly organized to help you set up your basic systems, and then do your best to maintain them.

4

No-Nonsense Principle Four:
Know Who Is Sitting in the Chair

"My sheep hear My voice, and I know them, and
they follow Me." John 10:27 (NKJ)

John Steinbeck was known to say, "Your audience is one single reader. I have found that sometimes it helps to pick your one person – a real person you know, or an imagined person – and write to that one." I can agree with him in the sense that a multitude is so much more difficult to visualize than a single individual when writing. We can continue to address information encompassing audiences with a few more questions. What is that one person – real or imagined – composed of? If you don't already know, then the search begins. What does he need that you can supply? What does he care about with an inquisitive passion? What would make him – your audience – appreciate you? The best way to discover this information and more is to go on a fact-finding mission of your own. Here are a few suggestions as to where to start:

Social Media is swarming with groups. It would be highly unusual for none of them to be concerned with your specific writing topic. If you want to find out what your prospective audience cares about, you'll have to join and participate. This may sound like it's not worth your time, but attempt to view your adventure as a two-fold opportunity. First, you can learn what most of your audience already knows about your particular topic. You needn't write what has already been established with your audience. Your job is to supply a new twist or idea. Second, you will be building your platform with every relationship you harvest through social media in general.

Platforming is necessary for every writer, no matter the topic or genre. The easiest way to judge the size of yours it is to ask yourself how many books you could sell today. Be realistic. A marginally successful writer has an answer in the 3,000 plus range. Do you know that many people? Can you guarantee each will purchase your book? Most of us have to work on platform.

Consider how you would go about estimating the number of folks who will actually show up for your annual Christmas party vs. the number invited. Let's say you sent fifty "Let's Celebrate Jesus Together!" invitations. Realistically, how many will walk through the door? You might be surprised to find out the average is 50%, but there is no tried and true rule because other factors exist. Your relationships with everyone you know could be so wonderful, nobody wants to miss your big event. And still, someone may become ill at the last minute, your pregnant guest may get a pre-Christmas gift and have to head to the hospital instead, or any number of other incidents could occur that decidedly effect your turn out in adverse ways.

The same holds true for book sales. People may sing praises and give you congratulatory hugs, then walk away from your book table empty-handed. While having the best of intentions, they may be in the worst financial season of their lives. That's why it is vital to build a platform. Your eventual goal is infinite, but start slowly. Each relationship you build is connected to many more relationships. Compounding works within your community if you handle your potential audience with care, love and respect.

Other relevant items about your audience are somewhat statistical. Age is a factor in almost every subject as it relates to language use. "Hip" language is only "hip" to the age range that recognizes the word. Within every topic are specific parameters to consider, such as income, aspirations and commonalities. Groups can help you identify what matters within a particular area. The same sort of statistic checks and balances hold true for faith. Not all Christians believe the same things, nor do atheists or people of other religions. It is your responsibility to avoid inadvertently offending others with your content or choice of words. This is the surest way to negate the credibility we discussed earlier. When I meditate on the scripture given at the beginning of this Principle, I always recognize that I am to hear His instructions in all that I write. He is in the business of increasing His flock through my work. If my work does not further His Kingdom, maybe I should reconsider what I'm writing.

Let's Review No-Nonsense Principle Four Self-Explorations

4.1 Writers tend to be accomplished at isolation, while struggling to step out into social scenes. The Internet was made for those reticent to physically show up for group gatherings. Net groups still take work on our parts. Building relationships, whether online or off, are give and give some more. If you don't interact, don't expect others to do what you aren't.

4.2 If you have limited skillsets in recognizing what others need, practice listening, listening and then, listening a bit more! People essentially love to talk about themselves if given the chance. The key is to ask open-ended questions, instead of those which can be answered with a monosyllabic yes or no.

4.3 We all feel more comfortable within a particular age range, but it's not always the one we currently inhabit. We can be gifted towards interaction with children, teens or the elderly, which opens the door to a writing niche. Writers who can look forward or back effectively often have the ability to speak to a generation about topics and in language that is appreciated and understood.

4.4 Storytellers tend to write fiction works. Problem solvers lean towards nonfiction. No edict is ever written in stone. The nonfiction writer is always called upon for anecdotes to carry a piece, which is nothing more than storytelling as well. No writer should feel restricted to one or the other, but it would be wise to establish yourself on one side of the fence at a time. As you may well recognize, the writing craft and nuances differ enough to matter. Also, the platforming demand is considerably higher should a writer attempt to do both simultaneously. After you build a house of fiction, then move on to your nonfiction abode, or the other way around.

5

No-Nonsense Principle Five:
Learn to M.O.P.

"Suppose one of you wants to build a tower. Won't you first sit
down and estimate the cost to see if you have enough money to
complete it?" Luke 14:28 (NIV)

No, I'm not talking about getting out the floor tools. M.O.P.
is an acronym that stands for Mind mapping, Outlines and Plans.
Every piece you write must contain more than a beginning,
middle and end. M.O.P. systems help you to connect necessary
points and solidify your thoughts on a topic.

A mind map can be a beginning brain flood. Start by
drawing a large circle in the center of a sheet of paper. Surround
the big circle with smaller circles. You'll record your main idea
inside the big circle. Example: Let's say you want to write a
piece about birds. Write the word "birds" inside the large circle.
Now you'll need to explore your voice and unique point of view
and place those ideas inside the smaller circles. What
information would you like to impart about birds? How to care
for them? How to bird watch? How to attract them to your
property? How to tell the difference between similar species? Let
your mind take you wherever it wants to go and fill in the tinier
orbs on the page.

From there, you can move to outlining your piece. This is
the time to organize and prioritize. Establish an order of
precedence so that your defined beginning, middle and end take
solid shape. Add more details under your subheadings that
continue to support what you have to say. Don't worry about
how long this process takes. Feel free NOT to include all of the

ideas on the mind map. Some of them simply may not fit into your emerging theme. The more material you include now, the easier the actual writing will be when you're ready to start your first draft.

Some writers actually brag about a lack of need for an outline. I always am reminded what the Bible says about such assumptions. The scripture, Isaiah 5:21 (NIV), cautions us about an overabundance of value and confidence placed upon our own egos. "Woe to those who are wise in their own eyes and clever in their own sight." Good writers are able to humble themselves to the rules of the craft. A mind map and outline create a much better story – be it fiction or nonfiction – than wisps of brain matter floating out of our heads at will. Creative flow coming from a wealth of preparation enriches our story lines to their absolute excellence.

The final step in our acronym sequence involves creating an action plan. Your plan should automatically imply deadlines and the sense of urgency you need to finish your project – regardless of an actual contract from a bona fide publisher residing in your file. Calendar your writing schedule into individual tasks that include not only writing, but research, editing and marketing allowances as well. Hopefully, you now see why we must be aware of our tendencies and habits. It doesn't accomplish much if I promise I will finish fifty pages of manuscript in one week if, in reality, I am a short burst, inconsistent writer. Discipline is the hardest battle any writer faces, and he cannot win it if he courts delusion and denial as his closest friends. Discipline is gained as a house is built. We must add one structural brick at a time. There is absolutely no shame in having a 250-word (or one typewritten page with one inch margins) starting goal. Think about writing 250 words daily for 365 days. That's a whopping 91,250 words! I've met very few writers who write every single day; however, I know many who arrange blocks of time regularly and assign a word count goal to those hours. To know yourself is to know how to M.O.P. your way to success!

Let's Review No-Nonsense Principle Five
Self- Explorations

5.1 If you are analytical and practical enough to consistently focus on a game plan, you are way ahead of most of us. I would caution this type of personality to schedule in periodic breaks away from your work. All of our projects need "drawer" time, where we walk away and think on other things. When we return, we are able to apply fresh eyes. The rest of us will have to pray, lay down appropriate boundaries with our friends and family and dig in. Focus wins the battle!

5.2 Many times a detailed action plan can look daunting. Start by looking for blocks of time within your daily agenda. At first, you may have to take what you can get. As you stack one brick upon another, you'll soon be willing to sacrifice other things in order to write. Sacrifice is generally unavoidable.

5.3 Envisioning the entire process may take some practice or even serious goal-oriented conversation with a mentor or critique partner. Your outline is an automatic guide to time sequencing, but don't omit research, editing and marketing from your planning.

5.4 Expect distraction and delay. The enemy already knows you've been given a mission with your pen. His greatest desire is to cause you to lose momentum and eventually give up. How many excuses have you heard from other writers about why they haven't been able to produce? How many of those excuses have you used? There are certainly situations when we are unable to write. It's interesting how rarely the valid reasons are quoted.

6

No-Nonsense Principle Six:
Pair with Precious Partners

"Therefore, since we are surrounded by such a great cloud of
witnesses, let us throw off everything that hinders and the sin
that so easily entangles. And let us run with perseverance the
race marked out for us." Hebrews 12:1 (NIV)

We, as both humans and writers, were never meant to
operate alone. God initially created us to have relationship, of
course with Him, but with others as well. Let's look at just a few
inspired instructions.

"For the body does not consist of one member but of many."
1 Corinthians 12:14 (ESV)

"Not neglecting to meet together, as is the habit of some, but
encouraging one another, and all the more as you see the Day
drawing near." Hebrews 10:25 (ESV)

"Whoever isolates himself seeks his own desire; he breaks out
against all sound judgment." Proverbs 18:1 (ESV)

Writing can be a solitary exercise. Most of us have already
seen late nights or very early mornings in front of a laptop.
We've experienced periods of self-isolation in an internal
struggle to wrestle an inkling of an idea, extend a plot or scrub
an outline. It is only in surfacing to interact with others that we

find out if we have accomplished our task. Haven't we always meant for our work to be shared? An instrumental key in getting into the published column is recognizing we are to share our manuscripts, not only in final pristine condition, but also in rough draft stages along the way. As in most situations that pertain to sharing, certain discernment is required. We don't need to pass out everything we write to everyone, demanding attention. There are appropriate places and people to include in your decisions. Here are some recommended community options.

God will always be first and foremost on the list, as it's not hard to take off on a flesh journey when we feel passionate about a topic. In more instances than not, flesh-oriented vocabulary (that not directed through the Holy Spirit) comes off preachy and authoritative. This author's delivery is traditionally susceptible to being considered in an offensive vein. Another indicator of this type of writing can be a severe use of what the industry calls the "Christian Cliché." Every Christian knows the phrase, "Jesus Saves," but almost no one is interested in hearing about it unless you can express intimate, passionate writing directed by God. Unfortunately, the flesh writer writes as though he **is** God, thereby destroying his own credibility in the eyes of any intended reader. Prayer and writing go as hand-in-hand as prayer and any other consideration you might put before our Lord.

Writing groups are necessary; however, they exist in various formats. My suggestion is to look for one physical group in your area that you can regularly attend. Pay attention to distinct meeting elements. Continue your search until you've obtained this tri-level objective: First, your group should have other writers you can interact with on a regular basis outside of group meetings. Second, there must be an environment of learning. You are attending to improve your writing. Last, there should be opportunities for you to share your work in a constructive critique setting. This is a primary way you can judge the response of a potential audience. As far as online groups are concerned – feast, as you will. There are competent groups on all of the major social media outlets. Just remember to absorb any information presented tentatively. You have almost no way of knowing the credibility level of those you are interacting with, and you should research thoroughly before you trust either an item or a source.

Mentors, critique partners and readers are give and take arrangements. It's unrealistic to expect a critique partner to work hard on your manuscript for a mere thank you and a smile. Be realistic by setting boundaries and guidelines for editing trade-offs. If you are unable to reciprocate, consider bartering other services or hire someone to edit your work. Mentors are in your life to contribute wisdom, more so than actual editing. Listen and heed their advice without arguing. Even if you don't agree, you've chosen to engage someone more advanced than you within the industry. Give them the respect they deserve. You will be a mentor someday, too!

Readers are invaluable for their opinions as non-writers. If you happen to run across a rare gem that simply loves to read, consider those individuals as gifts from God. Again, take care not to overwhelm or mistreat them. A gift card to a neighbor-hood bookstore will always be seen as a treat.

Let's Review No-Nonsense Principle Six
Self-Explorations

6.1 A prayer journal is never a bad idea. Write in the desires of your heart and then go back and record when God answers your prayer. Remember your dreams are God-given!

6.2 Not all of us have extrovert personalities, making it difficult for some to join physical groups. If this is you, I have some caring advice for you. GO ANYWAY. Try taking a buddy along until you feel more comfortable, but make the effort. Extroverts don't escape advice either. DON'T DOMINATE THE GROUP. It's more important to listen than to tell the group all about yourself and your writing history on your first visit.

6.3 Criticism is hard for beginning writers because they have a tendency to consider their projects as babies. Who would dare to slap a baby? It can be hard to separate your words from yourself. No writer ever improved without knowing what to keep and what to throw away. We need to learn what to stop doing and what to continue doing. Expect to gain that knowledge through taking the risk of divulging your work to other writers. Do you remember when you were learning to ride a bicycle? Do you still pine about the fall when you scraped your knees? After you accomplish a feat, the pain washes away. The same holds true with critiques. You'll learn to take them as they are intended if you submit yourself to the process frequently. And then your writing will improve!

6.4 Vulnerability and honesty are the traits needed to get the most out of group interaction. And it's also the place we least want to exhibit them. Practice saying, "I don't know." It's a statement with erroneous connotations in our society, but one of humility within writing groups. Using your own vulnerable state will glean you the information you need to move to your own next level.

Summing It Up!

These thirty or so pages seem to be shorter than I want them to be, but here we are at the end of the *No-Nonsense Manual*. Let's use these last two pages to summarize.

No-Nonsense Principle One is unavoidable. If you skipped it – go back! The better you know yourself, the easier it will be to find your particular writing niche, methods and style.

No-Nonsense Principle Two is worth plenty of experimentation. Write short pieces. Write a longer one. Next, see if the seed is planted within you to go to book-length work.

No-Nonsense Principle Three is a writer's version of spring cleaning. Throw out what doesn't work and form the new habits and routines you need to get where you want to go.

No-Nonsense Principle Four takes your focus off you and rightfully places your attention on your audience. Learn to write with at least one of them in the chair across from you always. I see **you** now!

No-Nonsense Principle Five issues your M.O.P. instructions with the intent of giving you a timeless structure that will never fail.

No-Nonsense Principle Six extends and expands your community in ways that will enrich your writing life and combat the isolation many writers tend to experience along the way.

Once again, it is my solemn hope and prayer I have created a fairly efficient overview of the writing life. The more you press in and seek information, the more you will be able to add to this tiny book.

May the Lord bless everything you write and may that work reach the audience He intended it to inspire.

7

Resources

BOOKS

On Writing Well	ISBN 0060891548
The Christian Writer's Market Guide	ISBN 1414387350
2014 Writer's Market	ISBN 1599637324
The Synonym Finder	ISBN 0446370290
Story Engineering	ISBN 1582979987
An Introduction to Christian Writing	ISBN 189252516X
The Heart of a Ready Scribe	ISBN 1462014399

BLOGS AND WEBSITES

www.faithwriters.com

www.christianwritersguild.com

www.goinswriter.com

www.thewritepractice.com

www.makealivingwriting.com

SCRIPTURES ON WRITING

"Your eyes saw my substance, being yet unformed. And in your book they all were written, the days fashioned for me, when as yet there were none of them." Psalm 139:16 (NKJ)

"My heart is overflowing with a good theme; I recite my composition concerning the King; My tongue is the pen of a ready writer." Psalm 45:1 (NKJ)

"Now go, write it before them on a tablet, and note it on a scroll, that it may be for time to come, forever and ever." Isaiah 30:8 (NKJ)

About the Author

      Melanie Stiles is a Christian Life Coach and author blessed with a rich freelance writing history. She has enjoyed hundreds of bylines, ranging from journalistic reporting to award-winning poetry. Her book, *The Heart of a Ready Scribe: 52 Reflections for Writers* has recently been awarded honors in both the 2012 Indie Excellence Awards and the 2013 Xulon Christian Choice Book Awards. As a frequent speaker at writers' conferences and women's venues, Melanie uses her background to instruct, inspire and celebrate life journeys with others. As a Christian Life Coach, Melanie is invested in helping not only writers, but all individuals to achieve the desires of their hearts. She would love to hear about your writing pursuits or life challenges. Simply email: Melanie@MelanieStiles.com.